CU00676331

Ministry of Defence

The Major Projects Report 2009

This volume has been published alongside a second volume comprising of –

Ministry of Defence: Major Projects Report 2009 Appendices and Project Summary Sheets

HC 85-II, Session 2009-2010

Ordered by the House of Commons
to be printed on 14 December 2009

Report by the Comptroller and Auditor General
HC 85-I Session 2009–2010
15 December 2009

London: The Stationery Office
£14.35

This report has been prepared under section 6 of the National Audit Act 1983 for presentation to the House of Commons in accordance with Section 9 of the Act.

Amyas Morse
Comptroller and
Auditor General

National Audit Office

10 December 2009

The Major Projects Report 2009 details the cost, time and performance of 30 military equipment projects from across the Ministry of Defence for the year ended 31 March 2009.

Printed in the UK for the Stationery Office Limited
on behalf of the Controller of Her Majesty's Stationery Office
P002337292   12/09   7333

Contents

The National Audit Office study team
consisted of:

Nigel Vinson, Andrew Makin,
Tim Bryant, Alison Taylor,
Matt Balding, Ben Bourn,
Sam Burford, Stuart Gardner,
Tom Halliday, Louise Hunter,
Simon Jones, Hannah Kingsley-Smith,
Richard Lewis, Michael Ralph,
Kelly Ross and Ashley Wain,
under the direction of Tim Banfield.

This report can be found on the
National Audit Office website at
www.nao.org.uk/mpr09

For further information about the
National Audit Office please contact:

National Audit Office
Press Office
157-197 Buckingham Palace Road
Victoria
London
SW1W 9SP

Tel: 020 7798 7400

Email: enquiries@nao.gsi.gov.uk

Summary

1   The Major Projects Report 2009 details the cost, time and performance of 30 military equipment projects from across the Ministry of Defence (the Department) for the year ended 31 March 2009.[1] The Project Summary Sheets, on which our analysis is based, are compiled by the Department and submitted by them to Parliament. Full copies of all the Executive Project Summary Sheets and Project Summary Sheets are available in Volume II[2] of this report and on our website.[3]

Conclusion on Value for Money

2   Two-thirds of the gross cost increases reported in the Major Projects Report 2009 reflect deliberate decisions to slip projects, taken corporately by the Department as part of a wider package designed to address a gap between estimated funding and the cost of the Defence budget over the next ten years. The size of the gap is highly sensitive to the budget growth assumptions used. If the Defence budget remained constant in real terms, and using the Department's forecast for defence inflation of 2.7 per cent, the gap would now be £6 billion over the ten years. If, as is possible given the general economic position, there was no increase in the defence budget in cash terms over the same ten year period, the gap would rise to £36 billion. In both cases these figures involve inevitably uncertain assumptions about the outcome of future Spending Reviews over a long period. In recent planning rounds, the Department concentrated its efforts on ensuring that the Equipment Programme was affordable in the early years, and on creating room in the budget for improvements in capability that were relevant to current operations. Since any radical changes in planned Defence capability would fall to be made in a Strategic Defence Review, the Department chose to make savings by re-profiling expenditure on existing projects and reducing the numbers of equipment being acquired on others. These decisions were necessary to ensure that the programme was affordable in the next few years, but they increased the overall procurement costs and represent poor value for money on the specific projects affected. The decisions did not (and could not) resolve the underlying issue of affordability which will need to be addressed by the Department, working with Treasury, as part of the Strategic Defence Review which is expected after the General Election.

3   Such corporate decisions make it difficult to conclude on the effectiveness of the delivery of individual projects by both the Department's staff and its commercial partners. It would be unfair to chastise those charged with delivering projects when the major drivers of cost increases lie outside their control. Indeed, on the performance of specific projects our analysis suggests signs of improvement in project cost control, with innovative decisions being taken to ensure progress. However, unless the Department addresses the underlying budgetary and governance issues it will not consistently deliver value for money for the taxpayer, or encourage its commercial partners to operate effectively. Nor, vitally, will the operational benefits of expensive new capabilities be available to the Armed Forces in a timely manner or in the numbers the original analyses suggested were required.

1   Our methodology is described in Appendix 1.
2   Ministry of Defence, *Major Projects Report 2009* (HC 85-II Session 2009-10), 15 December 2009.
3   www.nao.org.uk/mpr09.

Attempts to balance the defence budget in the short-term have increased overall costs on projects, and slipped the introduction or reduced capability, which represents poor value for money

4   The most pervasive feature of the changes in performance since last year's Report[4] is the effect of the Department's deliberate decisions to slip the introduction into service of some projects to produce short-term savings to address affordability issues. In particular:

- On the Queen Elizabeth Class aircraft carriers, the Department decided to slow the rate of manufacture to reduce forecast expenditure by £450 million in the next four years. After this time, costs are forecast to increase by a total of £1,124 million, giving a net increase in costs of £674 million. The decision causes the entry into service of the first aircraft carrier to slip by one year and the second by two years.

- On Astute Class submarines, the Department decided to slow the production of boats 2-7, which will lead to a net increase in forecast costs of £400 million, arising as a result of reducing expenditure by £139 million up to 2013/14. In addition, this decision is expected to result in a period between 2015 and 2021 when there will be a shortfall in submarines availability against the Department's stated requirement. As a result of the slippage on the Astute Class submarines, additional costs of £38 million will be incurred to continue running the existing, less capable, Trafalgar class submarines, although these costs should be at least partially offset by the (as yet unquantified) savings from not having to support the new Astute Class. Further extensions to the Trafalgar fleet are not considered feasible.

5   Of course, Government departments constantly make prioritisation decisions to commit to, or to defer, particular projects which are not yet underway depending on the available funding. These decisions may have an effect on the costing of the particular projects deferred because of underlying cost inflation. However in terms of the overall portfolio of projects the effects are generally compensatory. This logic does not apply to cost management by deferring a project by "slow down" once it is underway. This will typically drive substantial real cost increases into the project. This has been the case with some of the recent decisions taken by the Department, most notably on the Queen Elizabeth Class aircraft carriers. Whilst the decision to slip the aircraft carrier project has reduced average spend in each of the first four years by £112 million, it has increased the average annual spend for each of the next six years by £187 million. This adds up to a 16 per cent increase in the total cost of the procurement in order to obtain a spending deferral in the first four years, which looks an expensive decision.

6   The Department also generated savings by reducing helicopter numbers for the Lynx Wildcat and Merlin Mk2 fleets. The Department has taken a £194 million saving by reducing Lynx Wildcat numbers by 23 per cent, from 80 to 62 helicopters, and by reducing planned flying hours by a third. The Department has also decided not to proceed with upgrading the entire fleet of 38 Merlin Mk1 helicopters as planned; instead, only 30 will be upgraded. This will avoid £65 million of costs.

4   Ministry of Defence, *Major Projects Report 2008* (HC 64-I Session 2008-09), 18 December 2008.

7   The Department took these decisions as part of a wider package of savings to try to make the defence budget more affordable and to free up funding to support current operations. For example, the Department has been able to commit £330 million to provide a modernised set of equipment for training and engaging in close combat, including weapons and surveillance and target acquisition equipment.

These short term affordability decisions have combined with other influences to cause significant time, cost and performance variation

8   **Figure 1** shows aggregate time and cost performance for the 15 projects where the main investment decision has been taken. The current forecast[5] cost for the 15 projects that have passed their main investment decision is £60.2 billion, which is an increase of £4.5 billion (or just over eight per cent) compared to the expected costs when the main investment decisions were taken. The total slippage, when compared to the most likely In-Service Date, averaged across 14 projects[6], is 24 months per project.

9   Overall, the key changes to cost, time and performance on the 15 projects in-year are:

- Over £1.2 billion of cost increases (some 27 per cent of total cost growth since the main investment decisions were taken). The majority of this occurred on the Queen Elizabeth Class aircraft carrier (+£1,070 million), the A400M transport aircraft (+£653 million) and the Astute Class submarine boats 1-4 (+£192 million).[7]

- Excluding projects already in-service (Support Vehicles and the Typhoon aircraft, but not the Typhoon Future Capability Programme) an average slippage of seven months per project was added in 2009[8], compared to an average additional in-year slippage of six months in 2008. Five projects reported no change; and six projects slipped, including the A400M (+48 months), the Terrier engineering vehicle (+16 months), the Astute Class submarine boats 1-4 (+10 months), Queen Elizabeth Class aircraft carrier (+10 months), the United Kingdom Military Flying Training System (+8 months on two increments), and the Falcon communications project (+5 months on both increments).

- Seven of the fifteen projects are forecast to meet all of their Key Performance Measures without risk. Of 192 Key Performance Measures across 15 projects, 185 (96 per cent) are forecast "To be met". Twenty-one of the 185 are further assessed as "At risk"[9] across six projects, but the Department is confident it can mitigate these risks before the equipment enters service.

There are encouraging signs of improved performance in managing individual projects

10 There was a net increase in costs of £733 million in year as a result of the Department's decisions to slip the introduction into service of projects for short-term affordability reasons (referred to as Budgetary Factors in **Figure 2** overleaf). The associated gross cost increase was £1,046 million, or two thirds of the gross in-year cost growth. This was partially offset by a £313 million decrease. The remainder of the cost increases were mainly a result of Inflation or unfavourable Exchange Rates. These problems are not directly attributable to the actions of either teams managing specific projects or their delivery partners in industry. More encouragingly, costs over which project teams can exert more direct control – notably Technical Factors – have shown a net decrease in costs. Whilst performance by project teams in controlling time slippage has been more mixed, there has been no slippage on half of the projects in the last year. Taken together, these cost and timescale indicators suggest that project control has improved in 2009.

Figure 1

Time/cost performance for projects where the main investment has been taken

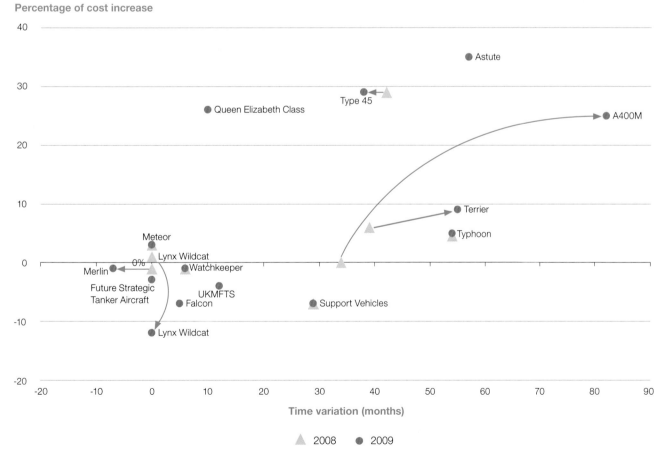

Source: National Audit Office analysis of Departmental data

NOTE

The arrows indicate in-year changes to cost and time performance since 2008. The Future Strategic Tanker Aircraft and Queen Elizabeth Class aircraft carrier are both new to this year's Major Projects Report; as such, no prior year figures are available. Astute Class submarines, Falcon and the United Kingdom Military Flying Training System all contain increments which were not reflected in last year's Report; as such, no comparable figures are available.

Figure 2

Most of the reasons for in-year cost variation reflect corporate short-term affordability measures, but slippage continues to be a problem at project level

Factor	Cost					Time				
	Gross Increase		Gross Decrease		Net	Gross Increase		Gross Decrease		Net
	(£m)	(%)	(£m)	(%)	(£m)	(months)	(%)	(months)	(%)	(months)
Project specific factors										
Changed Capability Requirement	9	0	-8	1	1	16	30	0	0	16
Technical Factors	61	4	-146	15	-85	15	28	-6	75	9
Procurement Processes	0	0	0	0	0	10	19	0	0	10
Receipts	3	0	-51	5	-48	0	0	0	0	0
Accounting Adjustments and Redefinitions	91	6	-469	46	-378	0	0	0	0	0
Sub-Total	**164**	**10**	**-674**	**67**	**-510**	**41**	**77**	**-6**	**75**	**35**
Other factors										
Budgetary Factors	1,046	66	-313	31	733	12	23	-2	25	10
Inflation	252	16	-3	0	249	0	0	0	0	0
Exchange Rate	120	8	0	0	120	0	0	0	0	0
HM Treasury Reserve	0	0	-20	2	-20	0	0	0	0	0
Sub-Total	**1,418**	**90**	**-336**	**33**	**1,082**	**12**	**23**	**-2**	**25**	**10**
A400M (classified)					653					48
Total					**1,225**					**93**

Source: National Audit Office analysis of Departmental data

NOTE

Commercial sensitivities mean this analysis excludes the A400M transport aircraft. An explanation of these factors can be found in Volume II and on our website www.nao.org.uk/mpr09.

Cost information relating to Typhoon has been declassified this year

11   For the first time since 2004 the costs relating to the procurement of the Typhoon combat aircraft have been declassified. This is thanks to the Department successfully concluding negotiations on Tranche 3A and reaching the financial ceiling agreed in the Memorandum of Understanding, which governs the project. The Department may, however, opt to purchase further Typhoon aircraft in the future.

The Major Projects Report is evolving

12   The Major Projects Report has traditionally focused on the procurement of new equipment and its format has not changed significantly since the Report's inception 25 years ago. In this time, the Department's approach to the acquisition of equipment and its support and delivery of defence capability has changed considerably. As such, the previous Major Projects Report no longer provided a complete picture to Parliament

of the evolution of the Department's current acquisition policies. The Department, with our support and the agreement of the Committee of Public Accounts, has made good progress in evolving the format of the Report.

13 The Report now details 15 projects that have passed their main investment decision with information, where appropriate, on each additional project increment. A new section covering Defence Lines of Development[10] (DLODs) has been added. The Report also includes details of a number of industrial contracts that have been put in place to support five significant in-service capabilities, and continues to provide data on ten projects for which the main investment decision has yet to be taken. These changes to the Report reflect a considerable commitment by the Department; further details on the changes can be found in Volume II and on our website.[11] Our Report this year includes some initial analysis of the new data. In future years, as the robustness of the underlying data sources improves and trends become apparent, we will undertake more detailed analyses reflecting the evolution of an equipment from the early Assessment Phase through to in-service support.

14 Looking further forward, the key development will be a new section with more extensive information on the cost and performance of in-service capabilities, rather than simply specific support contracts with industry. The Department is introducing Through Life Capability Management (including setting up Programme Boards) to ensure that new and existing military capability is planned and managed coherently across the DLODs. Through Life Capability Management should generate more reliable and robust management information than is currently available to support this reporting aspiration. However, its success is not assured and will depend on the Department addressing broader systemic factors such as the lack of a stable budgetary environment, whether the existing budgetary and organisational structures are appropriate, and the need to generate more robust and reliable management information. These are all factors which have adversely affected previous initiatives. Recognising these challenges, we assess that it will be at least two years before the Department will have sufficient, reliable and robust data and analytical tools to begin reporting detailed in-service performance and cost information to Parliament for non-equipment DLODs.

15 Following the publication in October 2009 of a report on Defence Acquisition by Mr Bernard Gray, the Department announced a range of planned measures to bring the equipment programme into closer alignment with longer term Defence strategy and the likely availability of resources, and to improve its overall governance, management and delivery. Among the main reforms are: a commitment to publish an annual assessment of the affordability of the equipment and equipment-support programmes against an indicative planning horizon for equipment spending agreed with the Treasury; and the introduction of better and more sophisticated techniques for forecasting project costs. It was also decided to establish a new sub-Committee of the Defence Board, chaired by the Accounting Officer, with a specific responsibility for developing an equipment plan that is aligned with strategy, affordable and realistic; this body has already begun work. A more comprehensive Strategy for Acquisition Reform is to be published in the New Year.

---

10 Defence Lines of Development are designed to assess the delivery of different aspects of capability, including: Equipment, Logistics, Training, Infrastructure, Personnel, Doctrine, Organisation, and Information.
11 www.nao.org.uk/mpr09.

Key Performance Measures			Platform Numbers		Notes and key developments in 2009
To be met	To be met, at risk	Not to be met	Approved	Current plan	
9	0	0	25	25	Significant slippage to in-service date
19	0	0	4	4	In-Service Date slipped and savings measure to slip the introduction into service of boats 2-7
7	0	0	Commercially sensitive	Commercially sensitive	Defences Lines of Development relate to In-Service Date 1, at which point no capability will be provided by Meteor
14	4	0	–	–	Slippage to In-Service Date and savings measure places two Key Performance Measures "At risk"
5	2	0	–	–	UK purchases three test aircraft and enters Operational Test & Evaluation phase
9	0	0	14	14	Final approval envelope set by investment approvals board in June 2008.
15	3	0	80	62	Savings measure reduces aircraft numbers to 62 from 80.
10	0	0	30	30	
9	0	0	2	2	Slippage on the introduction into service and cost increased
13	0	3	8,231	6,928	
8	3	0	65	60	Slippage on the introduction into service and three additional Key Performance Measures "At risk"
9	0	0	6	6	
15	1	1	144	144	Data relates to Tranches one and two
12	8	2	28	28	Platform numbers relate to Advanced Jet Trainer increment
10	0	1	54	54	
164	**21**	**7**			

Part One

Cost and timescale performance

1.1   In the first part of the Report we examine progress on the 15 largest equipment projects where the Department has already taken the main decision to invest (**Figure 3** overleaf). We also take a first look at five major commercial support contracts, which are included in the Report for the first time this year. **Figure 4** shows overall figures for in-year time, cost and performance for the 15 equipment projects, compared with Major Projects Report 2008.

Figure 3
The 15 largest equipment projects where the Department has taken the main decision to invest

In-year change to In-Service Date (months)	Current forecast In-Service Date	Expected In-Service Date at approval	Total cost variation (difference between current forecast and expected at approval) (months)	In-year change in Key Performance Measures: Not to be met	Defence Lines of Development			
					To be met	To be met, at risk	Not to be met	Not assessed
+48	Dec 15	Feb 09	+82	No change	6	2	0	0
+10	Mar-10	Jun-05	+57	No change	4	1	0	3
–	Aug-12	–	+12	No change	8	0	0	0
0	Aug-12	Aug-12	0					
0	Jul-15	Jul-15	0					
+5[1]	Nov-10	Jun-10	+5	No change	11	7	0	0
ISD excluded from analysis	–	–	–	No change	6	2	0	0
0	May-14	May-14	0	No change	5	3	0	0
0	Jan-14	Jan-14	0	No change	4	2	0	2
0	Feb-14	Sep-14	-7	No change	6	2	0	0
+10	May-16	Jul-15	+10	No change	7	1	0	0
In-Service	Feb-08	Sep-05	+29	No change	6	1	0	1
+16	Apr-13	Sep-08	+55	No change	8	0	0	0
-4	Jul-10	May-07	+38	No change	5	3	0	0
Aircraft In-Service	Jun-03	Dec-98	+54	No change	4	4	0	0
+8[1]	Jul-10	Sep-10	-2	+1[2]	7	1	0	0
0	Dec-10	Jun-10	+6	No change	3	5	0	0
+93			**+339**	**+1**	**90**	**34**	**0**	**6**

eight-month slippage across two increments.
Performance Measures across two increments.
not the "highest approved" boundary featured

Figure 3

The 15 largest equipment projects where the Department has taken the main decisi[on]

Projects	Description	In-year change on cost to completion (£m)	Current forecast cost to completion (£m)	Expected cost to completion at approval (£m)
A400M	Large transport aircraft	+653	3,285	2,628
Astute	Attack submarine	+192	5,522	4,102
Beyond Visual Range Air-to-Air Missile (Meteor)	Air-to-air missile: Original In-Service Date / Air-to-air missile: In Service Date 1 / Air-to-air missile: In Service Date 2	+3	1,282	1,240
Falcon	Deployable communication system	-7	331	354
Future Joint Combat Aircraft	Fighter/attack aircraft	-21	2,451	2,672
Future Strategic Tanker Aircraft	Air-to-air refuelling and passenger aircraft	-363	11,963	12,326
Lynx Wildcat	Light helicopter: battlefield and naval variants	-242	1,669	1,901
Merlin Mk2	Update of helicopter avionics	-2	830	837
Queen Elizabeth Class	Aircraft carrier	+1,070	5,133	4,085
Support Vehicles	Cargo and recovery vehicles and trailers	0	1,272	1,367
Terrier	Armoured engineering vehicle	+9	322	295
Type 45	Anti-air warfare destroyer	0	6,464	5,000
Typhoon	Fighter aircraft and Future Capability Programme	-54	17,962	17,115
UK Military Flying Training System	Flying training capability	-10	841	877
Watchkeeper	All-weather, 24hr intelligence, surveillance, target acquisition & reconnaissance unmanned air vehicle	-3	895	907
Total		**+1,225**	**60,222**	**55,707**

Source: National Audit Office analysis of Departmental data

NOTES

1   Falcon suffered the same five-month slippage on two increments, and the United Kingdom Military Flying Training System suffered

2   Advanced Jet Trainer previously reported a Key Performance Measure as "Not to be met"; this is now reported as two "Not to be me[t]

3   The "Expected costs to completion at approval" and the "Expected In-Service Date at approval" both reflect the "budgeted" foreca[st] most prominently in the Project Summary Sheets.

Corporate decisions to slip the introduction into service of projects for affordability reasons are the biggest cause of cost increases in the last year, but there are encouraging signs of better cost control by individual project teams

1.2   Figure 2 and **Figure 5** overleaf show that two-thirds (66 per cent) of gross cost increases in 2008-09 are due to Budgetary Factors, largely reflecting decisions made by the Department to reduce the short term cost of the ten-year Equipment Plan to try to make it affordable whilst reprioritising resources to current operations. We explore these programming decisions and their effect on individual projects such as the Queen Elizabeth Class aircraft carriers and Astute Class submarines in more detail in Part 2.

Figure 4

Headline figures for cost, time and performance of projects that have passed their main investment decision

	Major Projects Report 2009	Major Projects Report 2008
Total forecast cost	£60.2 billion	£45.1 billion
Number of projects	15 projects, with increments	20 projects, no increments
In-year cost increase	£1.2 billion	£0.1 billion
In-year slippage	93 months (average: seven months)	96 months (average: six months)
Key Performance Measures "To be met"	185 across 15 post-main investment decision projects, of which 21 across six projects are "At risk"	198 across 20 post-main investment decision projects, of which 16 across six projects are "At risk"
Key Performance Measures "Not to be met"	Seven, across four post-main investment decision projects	Seven, across five post-main investment decision projects
Defence Lines of Development "To be met"	124, across 15 post-main investment decision projects, of which 34 across 13 projects are "At risk"	(Not previously measured)
Defence Lines of Development "Not assessed"	Six, across three post-main investment decision projects	(Not previously measured)

Source: National Audit Office analysis of Departmental data

NOTE

Although forecast costs appear to have increased significantly since last year, two of the largest projects reported are new this year (the Future Strategic Tanker Aircraft and the Queen Elizabeth Class aircraft carriers). Also, for the first time project increments are included; later increments (which would typically have been outside of the Report's population) amount to £3.1 billion of forecast cost this year. Declassified Typhoon costs have been added back to last year's figures.

1.3 The other principal reasons for cost increases in the last year have been Inflation and Exchange Rates, over which individual teams have limited influence once projects are under way. Notably, there was an increase in inflation of £250 million on the Queen Elizabeth Class aircraft carriers because of higher than expected inflation on some of the raw materials and labour used to construct the ships. More encouragingly, costs over which project teams can exert more direct control have either been cost neutral or costs have reduced. For example, Technical Factors, which have accounted for considerable cost growth in previous years, reported a net decrease of £85 million in the last year (Figure 2). This performance reflects some good examples of project control and innovative practice (see **Box 1**).

Figure 5
Net cost increases of almost £1.3 billion masked widely differing results on individual projects

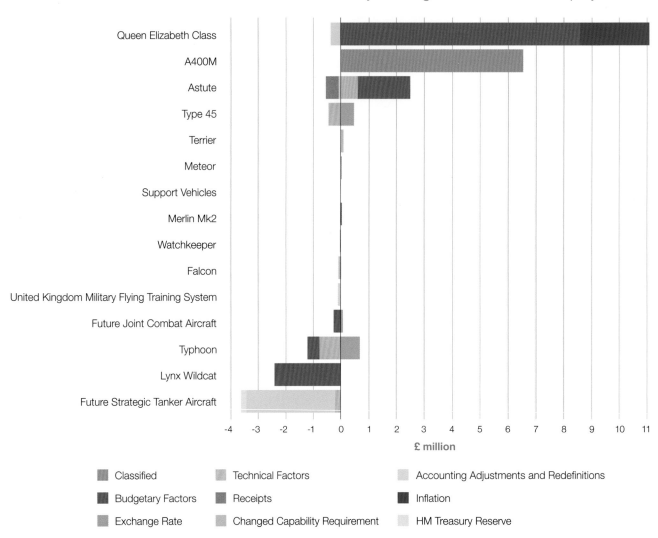

Source: National Audit Office analysis of Departmental data

NOTE
A400M breakdown of cost variations is classified.

Box 1
The Lynx Wildcat Helicopter

The Lynx Wildcat helicopter was developed to meet the requirements for a dedicated light helicopter for use by both the Royal Navy and the Army to replace the current Lynx fleet, which is reaching the end of its service life. Lynx Wildcat is a single-source helicopter procurement programme with AgustaWestland.

During the Assessment Phase, the Department and AgustaWestland jointly produced a Contractual System Requirement Document which provided a common baseline understanding against which to conduct commercial negotiations. The contract includes clear milestones and incorporates the use of Earned Value Management techniques to measure cost, time and performance in an objective manner.

The contract was signed in conjunction with a Strategic Partnering Arrangement, which encouraged joint working between the Department and industry. Key meetings are jointly chaired and common documentation including joint risk management, shared programme schedules and Earned Value data underpin both the Department's and AgustaWestland's governance processes. The teams have developed positive working relationships underpinned by regular and open communication, a common understanding of motivations and emphasis on improving people's personal behaviours. AgustaWestland has also cascaded these partnering principles to their sub-contractors using a partnering charter which encourages problems to be solved jointly.

1.4   Contracts to support five significant in-service capabilities are reported for the first time (**Figure 6** overleaf). In-year, there has been an overall decrease in costs of £274 million across the five projects. This comprises a reduction of £387 million in the forecast cost of Skynet 5, offset by an increase of £164 million in support to Tornado, resulting from increasing the planned flying hours from those specified in the contract to support current operations. The reductions in cost on Skynet 5 comprise a reduction of £387 million risk funding following the successful launch of the first three satellites. This risk funding covered the launch of a fourth satellite should any of the three satellites that form the constellation be destroyed on launch.

For the first time since 2004 Typhoon costs are publicly available

1.5   **Figure 7** on page 15 details all Typhoon cost variations since they were last published in 2004. The largest variation occurred in 2005, the first year of classification, and related to the removal of Tranche 3 from the forecast cost (-£978 million) and the separation of the first Typhoon Future Capability Programme into a new project (-£377 million). In 2007 a further amount was transferred out (-£482 million) to the second Typhoon Future Capability Programme. This project does not feature in the Major Projects Report as it has not yet entered its Assessment Phase. The first Typhoon Future Capability Programme was previously reported as a separate project in the Major Projects Report, but is now an increment accounted for in the overall Typhoon Project Summary Sheet.

Figure 6

In-year cost decreases on Skynet 5 are partially offset by additional planned spend to increase Tornado flying hours

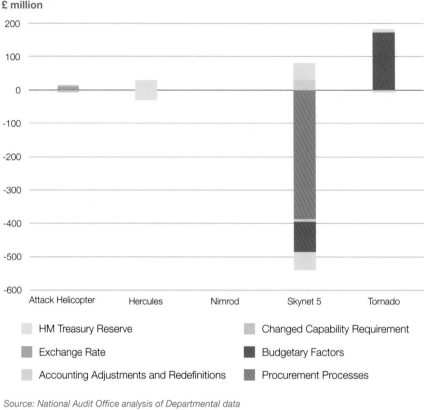

£ million

Legend:
- HM Treasury Reserve
- Exchange Rate
- Accounting Adjustments and Redefinitions
- Changed Capability Requirement
- Budgetary Factors
- Procurement Processes

Source: National Audit Office analysis of Departmental data

There has been significant timescale slippage in the last year

1.6 The 14 projects for which overall time performance can be reported[13] are forecasting to achieve their In-Service Dates, on average, 24 months later than expected when they were approved – a 26 per cent increase in their total expected timescales. Of this total slippage, an average of seven months has occurred in the last year.

Unlike for costs, the performance of individual projects in managing timescales remains patchy

1.7 As **Figure 8** on page 16 shows, six projects suffered slippage, and seven projects saw no overall change to their forecast In-Service Date in-year. The performance on the seven projects where there has been no change suggests improved project control on these projects, as the Lynx Wildcat helicopter example in Box 1 illustrates. The 10-month slippage affecting the Queen Elizabeth Class aircraft carriers reflects deliberate corporate decisions to slip the introduction into service of the project for affordability reasons. However, the reasons for slippage on the remaining five projects suggests schedule control remains patchy.

13 Excluding the Future Joint Combat Aircraft which does not yet have an In-Service Date.

Figure 7

Previously classified Typhoon costs have now been released

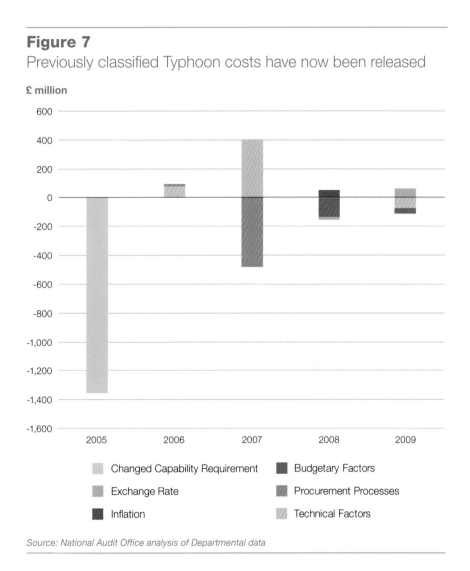

£ million

Legend	
Changed Capability Requirement	Budgetary Factors
Exchange Rate	Procurement Processes
Inflation	Technical Factors

Source: National Audit Office analysis of Departmental data

1.8   The 48-month slippage (taking the total on the project to six years) affecting the A400M transport aircraft accounts for over fifty per cent of overall in-year slippage. The contractor, Airbus Military, has already acknowledged that it underestimated the complexity of the project and its technical aspects, and these have caused the programme to slip its introduction into service. The cost escalation related to the slippage is predominately driven by Inflation, Exchange Rates and associated cost of capital changes, although the specific breakdown of these factors is currently commercially sensitive. In July 2009, the seven partner nations re-stated their commitment to establish a satisfactory way ahead for the project, and intensive work is continuing between partner nations and Airbus Military.

Figure 8

There has been slippage on almost half of the projects in the last year

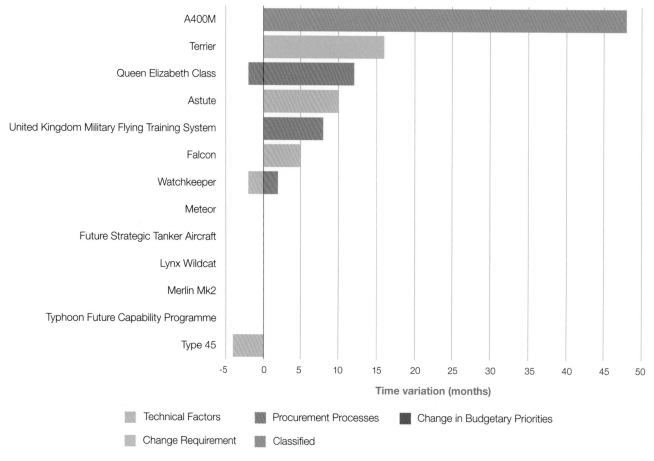

Time variation (months)

Technical Factors   Procurement Processes   Change in Budgetary Priorities

Change Requirement   Classified

Source: National Audit Office analysis of Departmental data

NOTE
Support Vehicles and the original Typhoon procurement (but not the ongoing Typhoon Future Capability Programme) are excluded as these projects have already entered service.

1.9 Since learning about the problems with A400M, the Department has been proactive in its response to addressing the capability gap caused by slippage on the project. The Department has studied its ability to sustain current and future operations, and has concluded that it should invest in a package of enhancement measures to maximise the use of the existing fleet of 24 Hercules C-130J aircraft. This includes additional infrastructure and enhanced contractor support.

1.10 The 10-month slippage on Astute Class submarines was caused by technical problems during the trials of the first boat. On the Falcon project there was also a five-month slip to the In-Service Date of each of the increments due to technical problems with the development of the telephony and encryption sub-system. Two of the United Kingdom Military Flying Training System's[14] increments suffered a slippage of eight months each, caused by slower than expected contractual negotiations.

1.11 During 2008-09 Terrier was subject to an additional slippage of 16 months. In September 2007, BAE Systems entered contractual default as a result of slippage in the production of the development vehicles and failure to demonstrate the required reliability on the prototype vehicle. In December 2008 the commercial agreement was amended to reflect a revised programme. During 2008-09, the Department has undertaken trading to incorporate lessons learnt on current operations. Specifically, it has opted to enhance the level of survivability (for example, improving mine blast protection) compared to that originally specified, and undertaken preparatory work for electronic counter-measures. The Department is also discussing with BAE Systems opportunities to vary the vehicle's weight and the length of time taken to perform digging tasks, in return for achieving the required reliability and durability. Although these opportunities have not yet been formally taken by BAE Systems, the Key Performance Measures related to digging have been placed "At risk". As a result of the above mentioned project adjustments, the Department has accepted an additional 16-month slip to the original In-Service Date, a reduction of five in the number of vehicles it is procuring, additional cost growth of £9 million and traded £7 million of liquidated damages from BAE Systems.

The capability required is largely expected to be delivered, although there are technical and other challenges to overcome

1.12 When the Department makes the main investment decision on a project, it approves a number (typically between nine and twelve) of Key Performance Measures (KPMs) which define the required capability of the equipment to be procured. Across the 15 projects that have passed their main investment point, 185 of the 192 KPMs are forecast to be achieved. Of these, 21 KPMs (11 per cent of the 185) across six projects are assessed as being "At risk" (16 across six projects in 2008). The Department still expects to achieve these KPMs, however, as risk mitigation strategies are in place.

1.13 Seven KPMs across four projects (seven across five projects in 2008) are forecast "Not to be met". The changes since last year's Report are because the Sting Ray torpedo Life Extension & Capability Upgrade (one KPM rated "Not to be met") has left the Report. The additional KPM forecast "Not to be met" this year relates to the simulated radar performance on the Hawk Advanced Jet Trainer – this has previously been reported, but now appears in two separate increments of the project as the Report now includes both Advanced Jet Trainer increments.

14 The project is designed to deliver flexible and integrated flying training for the Royal Navy, the Army Air Corps and the Royal Air Force. The project will take aircrew from initial training through elementary, basic and advanced flying training phases to their arrival at their designated operational aircraft.

1.14 Of the 21 KPMs which are assessed as being "At risk", eight relate to projects reported for the first time in Major Projects Report 2009, and ten reflect a change in assessment from last year:

- On the Falcon communications system two KPMs, (one relating to interoperability and one to survivability) common to both increments have been placed "At risk". This is as a result of an emerging requirement for integration with the Defence Information Infrastructure (Future Deployed)[15] that requires a technical change. Although integration with this specific system was not envisaged when Falcon's main investment decision was taken, the project's KPMs require Falcon to interface with other information systems.

- Three related KPMs are on the Lynx Wildcat helicopter, where, in a reassessment of priorities, the Equipment Examination removed the requirement for external fuel tanks on both variants. The Department states this will save £7.5 million, but the capability could be added back at a later date should there be a re-emergent requirement. Both variants have had their worldwide deployment KPM placed "At risk" because their range between refuelling has been reduced below the original level, which would result in self-deploying aircraft having to refuel more often. However, the Department would normally plan to deploy helicopters to theatre by strategic airlift, or, if time allowed, by sea. The naval variant has also had its surveillance capability KPM placed "At risk" because its endurance would be lower than the original requirement.

- Three are on the Terrier armoured engineering vehicle (see paragraph 1.11, above).

- Eight are on the United Kingdom Military Flying Training System. Given the immaturity of the later increments, the Department has assessed that all the overarching KPMs are "At risk", but is confident this situation will change as work to deliver the remainder of the United Kingdom Military Flying Training System progresses.

Defence Lines of Development are included in the report for the first time

1.15 The Department manages the introduction of military capability based on eight Defence Lines of Development (DLODs). This approach aims to ensure that all elements of a capability, such as Equipment, Training and Infrastructure, are introduced and managed coherently to meet current operational needs. For this reason, there may be a difference between the Equipment DLOD, currently expressed, and the KPMs reported in the previous section, which are set when the main investment decision is taken.

1.16 This year, for the first time, the Department has reported to Parliament the status of each of the DLODs for the 15 projects on which the main investment decision has been taken and the five projects with in-service support contracts. This is data the Department has not previously gathered centrally, and there is more work to do to ensure consistency of assessments and underlying data across the project population.

1.17 **Figure 9** summarises the data reported by the Department and shows that 159 DLODs across the 15 projects that have taken their main investment decision, and

---

15 Defence Information Infrastructure (Future Deployed) is the Department's secure information technology network which covers all three Services, including on-board ships and deployed on operations.

Figure 9

In the first year for which data has been reported, almost a third of Defence Lines of Development are "At risk"

Project	Equipment	Training	Logistics	Infrastructure	Personnel	Doctrine	Organisation	Information	Forecast In-Service Date as at 31 Mar 09
Hercules	●	●	●	●	●	●	●	●	In Service
Tornado	●	●	●	●	●	●	●	●	In Service
Attack Helicopter	●	●	●	●	●	●	●	●	In Service
Typhoon	●	●	●	●	●	●	●	●	In Service
Skynet 5	●	●	●	●	●	●	●	●	In Service
Support Vehicles	●	●	●	●	●	●	●	●	In Service
Astute	●	●	●	●	●	●	●	●	March 2010
Type 45	●	●	●	●	●	●	●	●	July 2010
United Kingdom Military Flying Training System	●	●	●	●	●	●	●	●	July 2010
Falcon Increment A	●	●	●	●	●	●	●	●	November 2010
Nimrod Maritime Reconnaissance and Attack Mk4	●	●	●	●	●	●	●	●	December 2010
Watchkeeper	●	●	●	●	●	●	●	●	December 2010
Falcon Increment C	●	●	●	●	●	●	●	●	February 2011
Meteor	●	●	●	●	●	●	●	●	August 2012
Terrier	●	●	●	●	●	●	●	●	April 2013
Lynx Wildcat	●	●	●	●	●	●	●	●	January 2014
Merlin Mk2	●	●	●	●	●	●	●	●	February 2014
Future Strategic Tanker Aircraft	●	●	●	●	●	●	●	●	May 2014
A400M	●	●	●	●	●	●	●	●	December 2015
Queen Elizabeth Class	●	●	●	●	●	●	●	●	May 2016
Future Joint Combat Aircraft	●	●	●	●	●	●	●	●	–

● To be met ● To be met, at risk ● Not assessed

Source: National Audit Office analysis of Departmental data

NOTES

Although 52 DLODs were forecast "At risk", only 50 are identified above. This is because Falcon also measures Interoperability (usually viewed as an overarching theme, and not separately assessed), which is assessed as "At risk" in both increments.

The data in this figure has not previously been gathered centrally by the Department and there is more work to do to ensure consistency of assessments and underlying data across the project population.

the five projects with support contracts, are expected to be achieved (94 per cent of the total) although of these, 52 DLODs across 18 projects are "At risk". The Department is confident that these will be met, as action is in place to mitigate the risks. The Nimrod Maritime Reconnaissance and Attack Mk4 aircraft has the most DLODs assessed as being "At risk" (all apart from Information), while Terrier and Meteor have no DLODs "At risk".

1.18 The most common DLOD to be assessed as "At risk" was Equipment. In eight of the eleven occurrences this was due to Technical Factors, for example, Falcon (see paragraph 2.14). Training, Logistics, Infrastructure and Personnel were all assessed as being "At risk" seven times with the main causes being Budgetary and Technical Factors. On the Typhoon aircraft project both Logistics and Training are "At risk" because the need to provide services to export customers of Typhoon has adversely affected the Department's ability to deliver these DLODs.

1.19 Eleven DLODs across six projects were not assessed. Four of these projects are already in-service; for example, the Tornado aircraft has been in-service for over 25 years but the Department does not have a benchmark against which to assess its Doctrine or Information DLODs.

Part Two

Corporate decisions on affordability have adversely impacted on individual projects

2.1   The Department's annual Planning Round aims to deliver a balanced and coherent Defence programme within the budget agreed with HM Treasury. As part of its planning process, the Department undertook an additional Equipment Examination in 2008 with the aim of reducing the cost of the ten-year Equipment Plan to make the Defence programme affordable, as well as rebalancing long-term equipment programmes to provide additional support to current operations.

2.2   The decisions taken in the Equipment Examination significantly affect five projects in the Major Projects Report. The projects most affected by slippage and short-term affordability decisions are listed in **Figure 10**, which shows the split between savings made in the next four years (which are harder to achieve as contracts have often already been signed) and savings made in later years. The cost, capability and other implications of the decisions are discussed in more detail in the following paragraphs.

Figure 10

Five of the Major Projects Report's equipment projects have been adversely affected by the need to balance the defence budget

Project	Variation in forecast equipment cost 2009-13	Variation in forecast equipment cost during subsequent years	Total forecast equipment cost variation
Queen Elizabeth Class aircraft carriers	- £450 million	+ £1,124 million	+ £674 million
Astute Class submarine, boats 2-7	- £139 million	+ £539 million	+ £400 million
Lynx Wildcat helicopter	+ £14 million	- £208 million	- £194 million
Merlin Mk 2 helicopter	£0 million	- £65 million	- £65 million
Falcon communications system	- £18 million	+ £42 to 67 million	+ £24 to 49 million

Source: National Audit Office analysis of Departmental data

The Defence programme is unaffordable

2.3 The Equipment Examination and subsequent Planning Round were successful in reducing the Defence budget's forecast overspend by £15 billion. The Department estimate, however, that the Defence budget remains over committed by £6 billion over the next ten years; this assumes an annual increase of 2.7 per cent in their budget after the end of the current Comprehensive Spending Review settlement in 2010-11. If the Defence budget remains flat in cash terms after this time, then the extent of the over commitment widens to £36 billion. In either case the budget remains consistently unaffordable over the next ten years (**Figure 11**).

2.4 Until there is a comprehensive review of defence policy, it will be difficult for the Department to think radically and rationalise the programme whilst limiting the impact on military capability. The Equipment Examination has also enabled the Department to shift some spending from future military requirements to support current operations (**Figure 12**).

Figure 11

Even after the Equipment Examination the Defence budget remains unaffordable

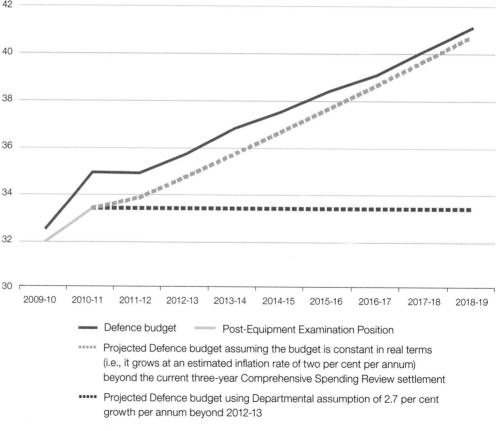

£ billion

Defence budget

Post-Equipment Examination Position

Projected Defence budget assuming the budget is constant in real terms (i.e., it grows at an estimated inflation rate of two per cent per annum) beyond the current three-year Comprehensive Spending Review settlement

Projected Defence budget using Departmental assumption of 2.7 per cent growth per annum beyond 2012-13

Source: National Audit Office analysis of Departmental data

Figure 12

The Department has made decisions to better support current operations

Project	Cost	Explanation
Dismounted Close Combat		
Tri-Service dismounted close combat consolidation	£330 million	Provides a modernised set of common equipment for training and engaging in close combat; including weapons and Surveillance & Target Acquisition equipment.
Helicopters		
Fit the Lynx Mark 9 fleet with T800 engines	HM Treasury Reserve: £73 million Departmental budget: £67 million	Fitting 22 Lynx Mark 9 aircraft with more powerful T800 engines will enable them to operate in the summer heat and altitude of Afghanistan. The first 12 helicopters are an Urgent Operational Requirement (funded by the HM Treasury Reserve to provide equipment for current operations). The remaining ten are expected to be funded directly by the Department once the business case has been approved. The Department expects the new engines to reduce the remaining through life costs of the Lynx Mark 9 fleet.
Merlin Mk3A Theatre Entry Standard	HM Treasury Reserve: £41 million Departmental budget: £9 million	This measure upgraded aircraft to Theatre Entry Standard, which increased aircraft availability in Afghanistan
Logistics Information Systems		
Management of the Joint Deployed Inventory	£86 million	This measure provided funding to deliver a timely and accurate logistics picture to operational commanders and improved asset management.

Source: National Audit Office analysis of Departmental data

Queen Elizabeth Class aircraft carriers

2.5 The Queen Elizabeth Class aircarft carriers were subject to an Equipment Examination decision which has increased the overall forecast cost of the project by £674 million. The overall pattern of cumulative spend before and after the decision was taken is shown in **Figure 13**. The primary aim was to constrain expenditure on the project during the four years commencing 2009-10 by slowing the rate of production. The Department expects this slowdown to yield a total reduction in spending of £450 million in the years to 2013-14. After this time costs are forecast to increase by £1,124 million. The net increase in costs of £674 million comprises £300 million of direct costs (for example, extending the design and engineering team by two years) and £374 million additional inflation due to the extended programme.

Figure 13

Short-term affordability considerations have increased the cost of the Queen Elizabeth Class aircraft carriers by £674 million

Queen Elizabeth Class cumulative effect of Equipment Examination

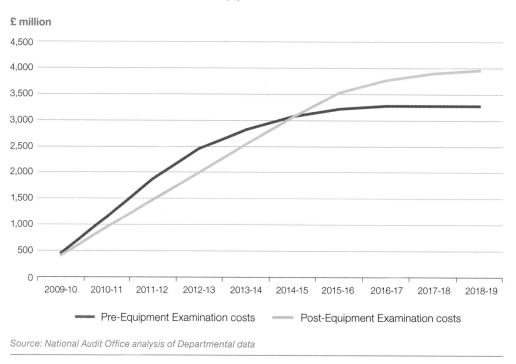

Source: National Audit Office analysis of Departmental data

2.6   The deferrals have also resulted in an increased cost of capital charge on the project of £234 million. The decision to constrain expenditure during the four years commencing 2009-10 will slip the entry into service of the first carrier by one year and the second by two years. To cover this delay, existing Invincible Class aircraft carriers will be extended in-service at an additional cost of £123 million, although these costs will be at least partially offset by the savings[16] from not having to support the new Queen Elizabeth Class aircraft carriers until their new In-Service Date.

Astute Class submarine

2.7   The Department made a similar decision on the Astute Class submarine, raising the overall forecast cost of the Astute Class submarine project by £400 million.[17] The overall pattern of cumulative spend before and after this increase is shown in **Figure 14** overleaf. The decision required the Department to constrain spending during the four years commencing 2009-10, by delaying the delivery of boats 2-4 and deferring the start of build of boats 5-7. The Department expects this slowdown to yield a total reduction in spending of £139 million in the years to 2013-14. After this time costs are forecast to increase by £539 million.

2.8   The decision to constrain expenditure during the four years commencing 2009-10 will not affect the first boat, but will slip the entry into service of each subsequent boat by an average of nine months. This is forecast to leave a period between 2015 and 2021 when there will be a shortfall of submarine availability against the Department's stated requirement. As a result of the slippage on the Astute Class submarines, additional costs of £38 million will be incurred to continue running the existing, less capable, Trafalgar Class submarines, although these costs should be at least partially offset by the savings[16] from not having to support the new Astute Class. Further life extensions to the Trafalgar Class fleet are not considered feasible.

Lynx Wildcat helicopter

2.9   The Lynx Wildcat project will provide light helicopters for both land and maritime environments, replacing the existing Lynx fleet which is reaching the end of its life. As part of the Equipment Examination, a decision was taken to reduce the number of helicopters being procured to 34 from 45 for the land variant, and to 28 from 35 for the maritime variant, an overall decrease of 23 per cent. The Department expects the reduction in the number of helicopters to deliver an overall saving of £194 million (10 per cent) in equipment costs over the next ten years, plus an additional reduction in the cost of capital. Further savings are expected to accrue from the associated decrease in the number of crews required to 72 from 110 and in support costs over the life of the fleet.

---

16   These savings have yet to be quantified.
17   Major Projects Report 2009 Astute Project Summary Sheet only reports on the progress of boats 1-4, the builds of which have already commenced. The cost of delaying these totals £189 million.

Figure 14

Short term affordability considerations have increased the cost of the Astute Class submarine by £400 million

Astute boats 2-7 cumulative effect of Equipment Examination

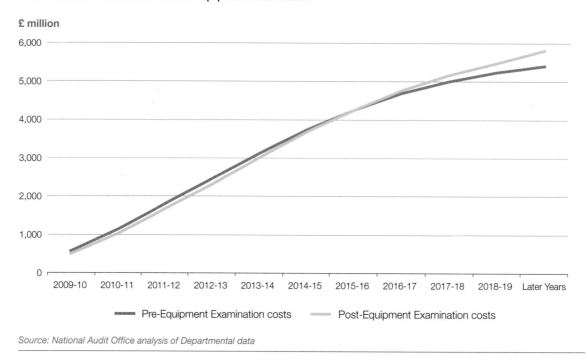

Source: National Audit Office analysis of Departmental data

2.10 Decisions to reduce helicopter numbers to remain within a project's cost approval or generate wider savings can be economically inefficient when considered in isolation. Although the decision saved 12 per cent of the Lynx Wildcat's costs, it represented a 23 per cent reduction in helicopter numbers.

2.11 The planned number of Lynx Wildcat flying hours has also been reduced by a third. The Department will mitigate some of the capability risk the reduction in airframes brings by increasing simulator hours, having a common training solution for the two variants, and through operating all aircraft from a single base. The Department did not undertake formal operational analysis on the impact of the reduction; rather it based its assessment on military judgement that the reduced numbers would be sufficient to meet military tasks.

Merlin helicopter

2.12 The Merlin Capability Sustainment Programme is designed to upgrade Mk1 standard helicopters to the Mk2 standard to support anti-submarine and maritime operations. The upgrade will overcome obsolescence issues and sustain the helicopter until its planned 2030 Out-of-Service Date. The Equipment Examination resulted in the Department not proceeding with the plan to upgrade the entire fleet of 38 Mk1 helicopters. Instead, only 30 will be upgraded. This reduction will avoid £64.7 million of costs.

2.13 As a result, the Merlin force will be unable to provide simultaneous anti-submarine protection to more than one naval task force, such as an aircraft carrier or amphibious group, unless supplemented by Merlin helicopters used for training.

Falcon communications project

2.14 Falcon is a high capacity system that is designed to link tactical communication networks. It will allow for rapidly deployable, secure voice and data communication links at all levels of command. During the Equipment Examination, a decision was taken to withdraw funding for an emerging requirement for interoperability with Defence Information Infrastructure (Future Deployed) that would have cost £18 million[18]. This emerging requirement has had the effect of putting the Interoperability and Survivability KPMs "At risk". If Falcon is to deliver the intended operational benefits and meet all its KPMs these integration activities will still need to take place. Initial cost estimates from industry indicate that carrying out these activities at a later date may cost between £42 million and £67 million, although the Department expects the actual cost to be lower.

18 The Falcon Project Summary Sheet currently only shows the first year's costs of £8 million removed from the project at the reporting date of 31 March 2009. Later year's costs of £10 million are expected to be removed in the near future.

Part Three

Improving the measurement and management of military capability

3.1 The Major Projects Report has traditionally focused on the procurement of new equipment. Building on the changes already made to the format of the Major Projects Report, notably the inclusion of in-service support contracts and assessment of achievement against DLODs, the Department has committed to provide information on the in-service performance and costs of equipment.

3.2 Since 2007, the Department has been undertaking a major long-term change programme, called Through Life Capability Management (TLCM), to implement a more effective way of providing military capability to the frontline. TLCM is defined as: "an approach to the acquisition and in-service management of military capability in which every aspect of new and existing military capability is planned and managed coherently across all Defence Lines of Development (DLODs) from cradle to grave." Correctly implemented, TLCM should generate more reliable and robust management information than is currently available, which could form the basis of future reporting to Parliament on the cost and performance of in-service equipment. This Part of our Report assesses the Department's progress in introducing TLCM.

Through Life Capability Management aims to improve the effectiveness with which the Department meets military requirements

3.3 The principles underpinning the move to TLCM are sound and, if they can be introduced successfully, the potential cost and operational benefits are significant. TLCM should:

- ensure that there is coherence across all the DLODs as new capability enters service;

- manage risks to current capabilities and assess whether future capability needs would be best served by upgrading existing equipment or investing in new equipment;

● match resources to the available funding, and identify opportunities to improve capability and value for money by trading resources between projects or across DLODs; and

● identify efficiencies and opportunities for greater coherence, for example, by projects sharing common training facilities, infrastructure or supporting technology.

3.4 A key element of TLCM has been the introduction, progressively since autumn 2008, of Programme Boards. The Programme Boards are responsible for translating capability plans into specific outputs, which are delivered to the front line commands. Each Board is led by the relevant Head of Capability, and includes representatives from the front line command, those responsible for delivering each of the eight DLODs, the finance function and, where it is felt to be appropriate, industry. The Department's approach has been to introduce the Boards quickly and to use central design and implementation teams to help develop the underlying processes, support and decision-making networks in parallel, learning from emerging experience. All the Programme Boards were established by April 2009, and had met by August 2009.

3.5 Given the pace of implementation and the variety of capabilities being managed, it is not surprising that we found some divergence in the approaches and activities of the Programme Boards. However, we did find encouraging signs that by bringing key decision-makers together more coherent judgements are being made. **Figure 15** overleaf shows how the Unmanned Aerial Systems Programme Board is managing a mix of in-service equipments, those still in development and manufacture and those acquired as Urgent Operational Requirements. For example, the Board is seeking to maximise the reuse of Watchkeeper infrastructure facilities to support the next generation of unmanned aerial vehicles, thus potentially avoiding cost duplication. The scale of the potential future cost avoidance is being calculated but, indicatively, the initial cost of acquiring the Watchkeeper training facility is some £30 million.

The Department recognises that much remains to be done to fully develop Through Life Capability Management

There are gaps in management information

3.6 Securing the cost and operational benefits of TLCM will not be easy, as experience from previous attempts to introduce similar, less wide-ranging, initiatives in the past shows.[19] From the perspective of the proposed evolution of the Major Projects Report, the key challenge facing the Department is the generation of sufficient, robust and timely information upon which to make well-founded decisions.

---

19 For example, the 2000 Smart Acquisition included a whole-life approach to equipment procurement and support, in theory typified by applying "through-life costing techniques".

Figure 15
The Unmanned Aerial Systems Programme covers projects at different stages of the acquisition lifecycle

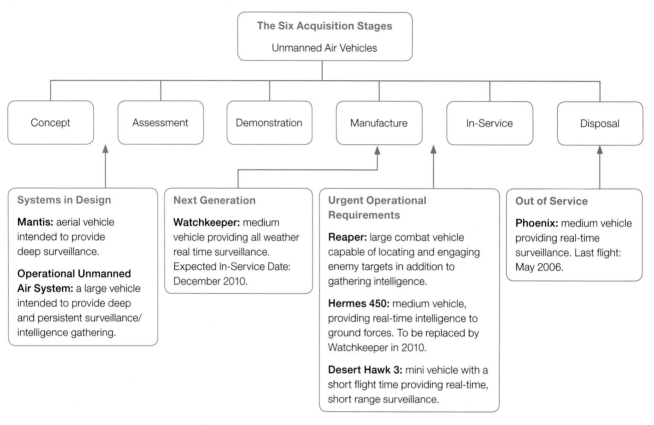

Source: National Audit Office presentation of the Department's material

NOTE

Deep surveillance: Long range surveillance, far behind enemy lines.

3.7 Previous initiatives have emphasised the importance of whole-life costs, but the Department has faced challenges generating robust and consistent information. The Programme Boards do not currently have good information on the overall costs of their programmes across all DLODs, which adversely affects their ability to explore balance-of-investment trading opportunities. By March 2010, the Department plans to develop a tool for collating and presenting consolidated financial data on the planned Equipment and Logistics DLODs' costs of programmes over the next ten years. The Department has also considered how it might improve financial data available on the other six DLODs' but has not yet set a target for when better data will be available.

3.8 The Department is developing its existing reporting tools so that, by March 2010, it should be able to generate a consistent set of non-financial information, for example, on programme level risks and dependencies, and on progress against DLOD plans. The Department recognises that the DLOD owners, with help from the Programme Support Functions, will need to address current weaknesses in underlying processes and data if the new tools are to provide good quality information.

3.9 Generation, collation and analysis of much of the data will be undertaken by Programme Support Functions aligned to the Programme Boards. These Programme Support Functions are fully staffed through a combination of permanent posts and support from within Defence Equipment & Support's Operating Centres.

There are other systemic issues to address

3.10 There are other systemic influences which the Department needs to address if it is to make TLCM a success. These include:

- **The lack of a stable budgetary environment.** Where opportunities are identified to improve value for money and deliver better capability by trading resources between DLODs or projects, the availability of sufficient funding, particularly where it involves near term spend-to-save measures, is likely to be limited. Until the Department has a stable defence programme, opportunities for trading will remain constrained, and could erode support within the Department for the TLCM approach.

- **Programme Boards cut across the Department's existing budgetary and organisational structures.** Both we and the Committee of Public Accounts have commented on the challenges existing Departmental structures pose for the coherent delivery of capability.[20] Initially at least, the Department has decided that Boards should not hold the funding for their programmes, although representatives of those who do hold the budgets sit on the Boards, as do representatives from the central finance community. The Heads of Capability who chair the Boards hold the equipment and equipment support funding for future projects and it is around this financial data, rather than information on all of the DLODs, that the operation of the programmes is currently coordinated. As the Department gains experience in operating Programme Boards, it will need to assess whether Boards have sufficient authority to allocate programme resources across the existing budgetary structures, and direct activities to improve the efficiency and effectiveness with which they deliver capability.

- **Securing full support from all parts of the Department and its industry partners.** The Department recognises that engagement of front line commands will need to improve if TLCM is to be successful. A major effort is currently underway by the Department to assist front line commands in integrating the TLCM approach into their established ways of working and improve their management of DLODs, for example, by providing new project management training courses. We have also noted differing approaches to the extent and timing of industry involvement in discussions.

20   See Committee of Public Accounts, *Ministry of Defence: Delivering digital tactical communications through the Bowman CIP programme*, HC 358, Fourteenth Report, Session 2006-07, pp 9-10.

Appendix One

Methodology

The Major Projects Report 2009 is the twenty-sixth to be produced by the Department. The Committee of Public Accounts originally requested the Report after their 9th Report, Session 1981-82, which noted the absence of any requirement for the Department to inform Parliament about the costs of its major military projects.

The Major Projects Report is not a statutory account, and we do not offer a formal audit opinion on the accuracy of the data contained within it.

Selected Method	Purpose
1 Evaluation of individual projects	
We examined 30 projects (15 of which have passed the main decision point, 10 of which have not, and five of which are in-service) to assess cost, time and performance. The resulting Project Summary Sheets are compiled according to agreed guidelines.	To confirm that the Project Summary Sheets conform to the guidance and that it has been accurately and consistently applied. We do not question forecasts or assumptions of the Department's long term costings unless better information becomes available.
2 Review of key documents	
Our review included key Departmental planning documents, contracts, project plans, contractor reports, and assessments of performance by the Director of Capability and front line commands.	To validate the information provided by the project teams in the Project Summary Sheets.
3 Semi-structured interviews	
We interviewed staff from the Ministry of Defence, including:	To identify and validate the time, cost and performance information contained in the Project Summary Sheets.
● The 30 project teams,	
● Director of Capability,	To understand the context of this information and the decisions the Department have taken.
● Heads of Capability,	
● Defence Equipment and Support directors,	
● Defence Lines of Development owners, including front line commands.	

Selected Method	Purpose
4 Analysis of cost, time and performance	
Using the qualitative and quantitative data collected above, we considered whether the Department is forecasting to deliver to the budget, time and performance expected when the main investment decision was made.	To identify the greatest cost and time variances and the factors that cause them, with particular attention to trends in the Department's overall performance.
Interest Rate Calculation: we used the internal rate of return method to calculate the annual interest rate required for the benefit of delaying a project (cost savings in the first few years) to equal the cost of the delay (cost increases in later years).	This allows us to demonstrate the cost of delaying a project in a more meaningful way.

Appendix Two

Assessment Phase Projects

Prior to the main investment decision being made, forecast costs are for internal planning purposes only. Publicly declaring these costs limits the Department's ability to make trade-offs and conclude satisfactory commercial arrangements. These costs are classified but disclosed to the Committee of Public Accounts to maintain public accountability. **Figure 16** shows the approved and forecast cost of each Assessment Phase.

Figure 16
Cost of the Assessment Phase

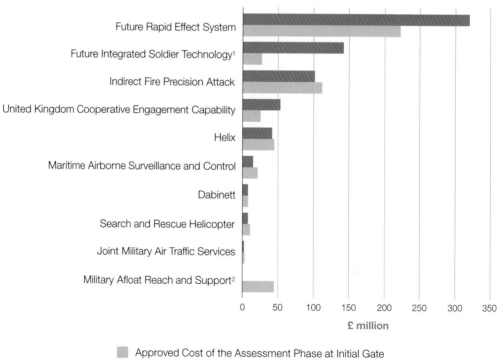

£ million

Approved Cost of the Assessment Phase at Initial Gate
Forecast Cost of the Assessment Phase

Source: National Audit Office analysis of Departmental data

NOTES
1 The forecast cost for Future Integrated Soldier Technology is for Assessment Phases 1-3. The approved cost is for Assessment Phase 1 only.

2 The forecast cost of the Assessment Phase for the Maritime, Afloat, Reach and Support has been classified as the information is commercially sensitive.

Appendix Three

Support Projects

Although some individual approvals, such as the Hercules support contract, are approved at the "not to exceed" level, the Department continues to plan on the basis of the "most likely" or expected cost. Therefore, the approval figures below represent the "most likely" forecast approved to ensure comparability across each of the support projects. This is calculated by deducting the "Risk Differential" factor within a support projects' Project Summary Sheet to arrive at the "most likely" figure (**Figure 17**).

Figure 17
Cost of Support Contracts

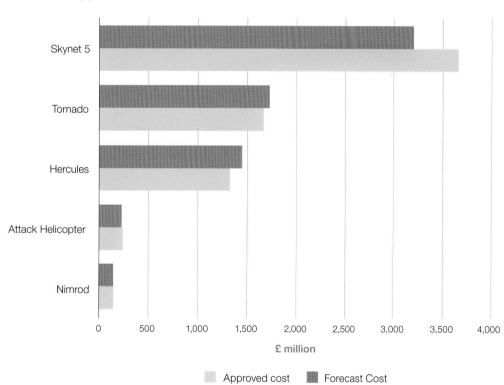

£ million

Approved cost   Forecast Cost

Source: National Audit Office analysis of Departmental data